The Horse

Christopher Wynne

Prestel
Munich · Berlin · London · New York

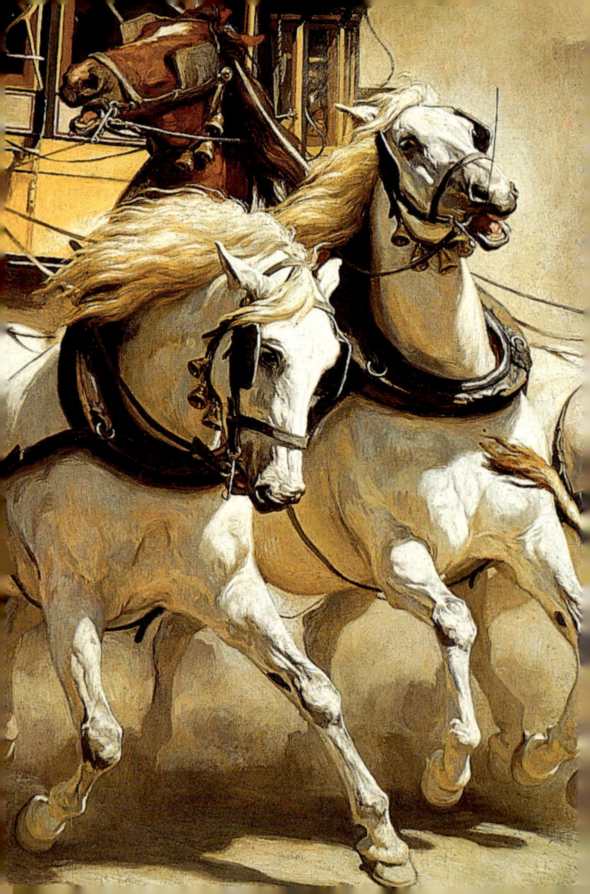

"A horse! A horse! My kingdom for a horse!"

No other animal has been depicted in works of art as frequently as the horse, and no other animal has played such a crucial role in the evolution of humankind. Admired for their strength, speed and intelligence, horses have not just been our most faithful companion in peacetime and in war, but have long been seen as a symbol of power and majesty. Richard III was prepared to sacrifice everything for a noble steed whereas, elsewhere, the animal's magnificence is expressed more prosaically: "Horse, thou art truly a creature without equal; for thou fliest without wings and conquerest without sword."

Since time immemorial the influence of the horse on all aspects of life has been reflected in the art of the world's great cultures. The oldest work of art depicting a horse is a small sculpture made of mammoth tusk. Discovered in present-day Germany, it is believed to have been carved 30,000 years ago, and predates the world-famous cave paintings in France and Spain. Created at a time when prehistoric man still regarded horses purely as a source of food, the animals depicted in the cave paintings closely resemble the Przewalski horse, a wild breed first discovered in Mongolia that still survives to this day.

The history of the horse, however, goes back much further. Fifty-five to forty-five million years ago, 'eohippus' (dawn horse) appeared on Earth. It was no bigger than a dog, but it would gradually evolve into the first, single-toed (or hoofed) animal. Only in the last two million years did it develop into the horse that we know today, and it was not until around 4000 B.C. that, on the steppes to the north of the Black Sea, first attempts were made to domesticate it. Initially used as a mere beast of burden by nomadic tribes, horses were soon put to work in the first fields ever ploughed. Once the art of riding had been mastered, hunting became easier, great distances could be covered and new regions explored. Battles were no longer fought on the ground but won on horseback. And with the invention of the wheel, horsepower took on a whole new meaning.

In Homer's *Iliad*, one of the oldest literary documents of western civilization, horses were created by the gods themselves and seen guiding the chariots of their masters to glory both in war and in races held on the plains of Troy.

Myths and legends of horses abound. Poseidon, the God of the Sea, frequently disguised himself as a stallion; Arion, the wild horse, had both the power of speech and the front feet of a man, whereas Pegasus, the winged steed, and creatures such as the unicorn and the centaur, transported the horse into a magical realm. Ancient man endowed the noble beast with god-like attributes, and mighty steeds were credited with drawing the sun across the skies.

From chariots of war to competitions at the early Olympics in Greece, the horse advanced from the battlefield to the racetrack. Similarly, in the Orient, the Chinese quest to maintain its equestrian strength led to a series of military campaigns in search of superior horses. These expeditions forged links between the East and West and resulted, ultimately, in the opening of the famous Silk Road. It was also the Chinese who produced three of the most significant inventions in equestrian history: an effective harnessing system, the stirrup and the horse collar.

Painted on pottery and moulded in terra cotta, cast in bronze and woven in tapestries: the horse has been depicted in virtually every conceivable way. However, it was not until the seventeenth century that horse painting emerged as a distinct genre. The Dutch artist

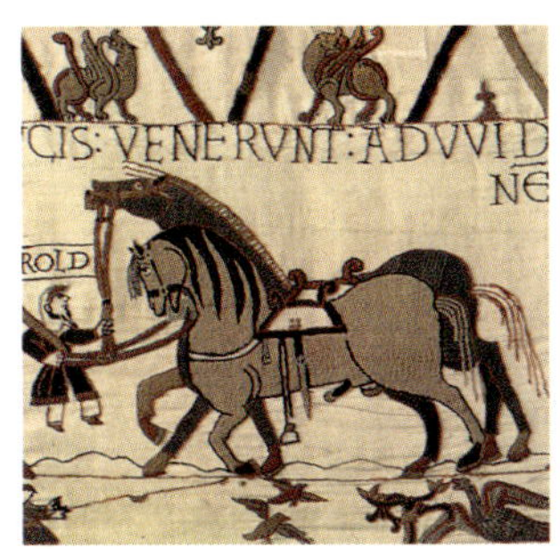

Detail from 'The Bayeux Tapesty', *c.* 1070

Paulus Potter (1625–54; p. 16) particularly influenced the way animals were depicted in European art. He painted portraits of horses and made them the focus of his work rather than accessories to human activities. He developed a strong feeling for composition and paid scrupulous attention to detail.

This is equally true of George Stubbs (1724–1806), the most famous horse painter of all time. His canvas *Mares and Foals* (pp. 14/15) shows perfect animals in an ideal setting. This quintessentially English artist, however, could never have achieved such perfection without careful scientific observation. In 1766 Stubbs published *The Anatomy of the Horse* after spending eighteen months dissecting, analysing and drawing the animal's muscle and bone structure.

Progressing from early hunting scenes executed in a traditional style, Stubbs brilliantly demonstrated his knowledge and skill in his famous paintings of racehorses. The portrait of Gimcrack (p. 35), like many similar paintings by Stubbs, follows in the tradition of earlier British artists such as John Wootton (1682–1765; p. 33). In these works, however, Stubbs displays his superior grasp of anatomy and painterly prowess to good advantage. Unlike Potter, Wootton and other major animal painters, Stubbs' horses are not necessarily embedded in a landscape as part of the overall composition. In fact Stubbs often painted the background only after he had completed the portrait of the horse. In *Hollyhock* (p. 17), the landscape was even added later by two French artists, and in many of Stubbs' works painted in the 1760s, the background is missing altogether. In the life-sized portrait of *Whistlejacket* (pp. 18/19) no landscape detracts from the strength and vitality of this magnificent horse, commissioned at a time when his racing days were already over.

The horse portraits painted at the beginning of the eighteenth century by the Flemish artist Johann Georg von Hamilton (1672–37; pp. 20/21) were also executed with considerable precision. The two imposing, highstepping stallions of Italo-Hispanic origin, with long manes and tails and handsome Roman noses, came from the famous Eisgrub stud.

Proud owners and breeders throughout the centuries have commissioned paintings of their champion thoroughbreds – horses whose

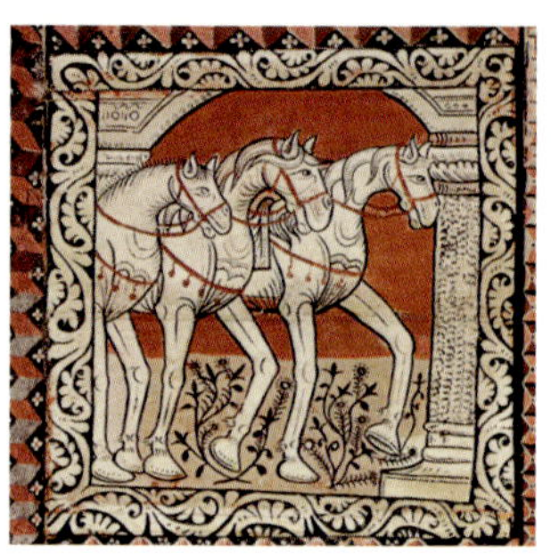

The Horses of the Three Kings,
early 12th century.

ancestry can be traced back to the three foundation sires: the Byerly Turk, the Darley Arabian, foaled in Syria, and the Godolphin Arabian, bred in Yemen. Named after their respective owners, these three stallions were brought to England in the late seventeenth and early eighteenth centuries to breed with the stronger, native horse. This selective breeding process has been continued to this day, with the proof of superiority and excellence being established on the racetrack. Some artists, such as Albrecht Adam (1786–1862; pp. 22/23), included figures in traditional or oriental dress to emphasize where the thoroughbreds had been acquired.

Photography brought about a radical change in horse painting. The English photographer Eadweard Muybridge (1830–1904), who emigrated to the USA in 1851, was a pioneer of the moving image. In 1878 he published his series of pictures *The Horse in Motion.* These photographs document the movement of a horse's legs when trotting and galloping and were avidly studied by animal artists around the world.

Théodore Géricault's painting of a horse race (pp. 36/37) was completed in 1821, long before Muybridge's discovery. Unlike Henri de Toulouse-Lautrec's painting *The Jockey* (p. 34), Géricault's horses are still depicted with all four legs outstretched. His sketches (p. 28), however, like his powerful painting of a horse's head (p. 27), brilliantly capture the essential nature of the horse, and greatly influenced other contemporary artists such as Eugène Delacroix (p. 29).

The tradition of commissioning paintings of racehorses still continues. Paintings by Alfred Munnings (1878–1959), the greatest, British, equestrian painter of the twentieth century, now command top prices at auction. Although most famous for his racecourse scenes and his portraits of thoroughbreds, Munnings did not regard his commissioned works to be his best, preferring instead to paint and sketch subjects of his own choice, free of any constraints. His expressive sketches and paintings of Exmoor ponies (pp. 54/55), for example, reflect his love of the countryside and its wildlife. The hardy Exmoor pony, an ancient breed of wild horse, still survives in small herds on the open moorland of West Somerset and North Devon.

Countless artists, including Munnings, painted everyday scenes of working horses in all their facets. Whether brewery drays or shire horses, street scenes of hansom cabs in New York (p. 48) or post coaches on mountain passes (p. 49), horses dominated rural and city life well into the twentieth century.

That most noble of animals has never ceased to capture the imagination of artists throughout the centuries. The close bond between man and horse, evident in works of art around the globe, and our fascination for the horse will ensure it is also given a special place in the world of art in years to come.

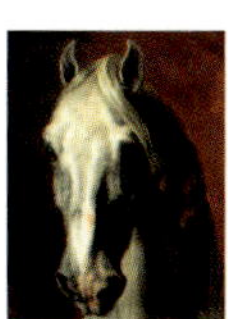

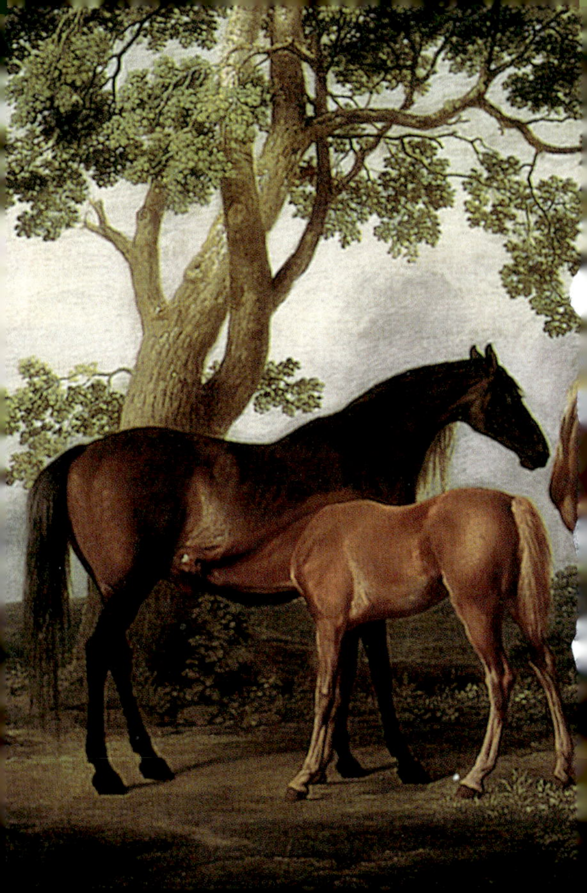

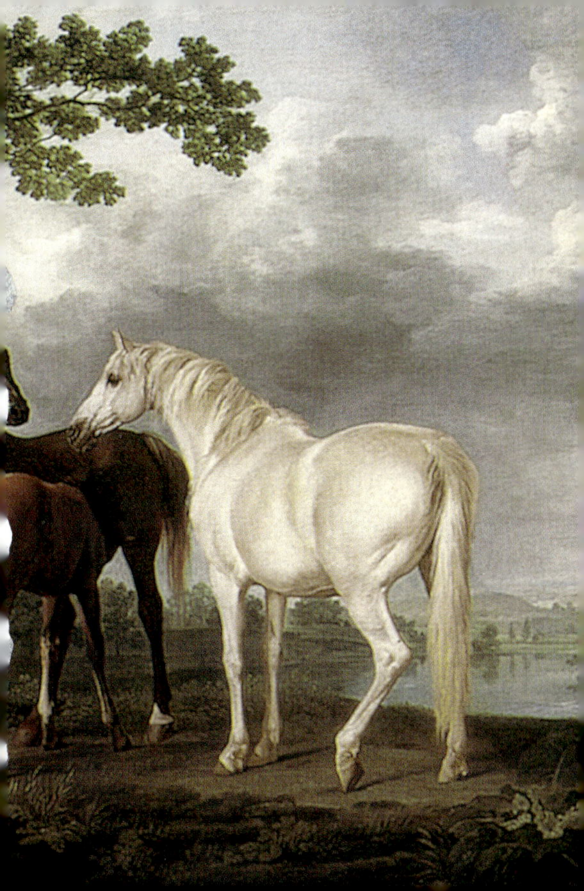

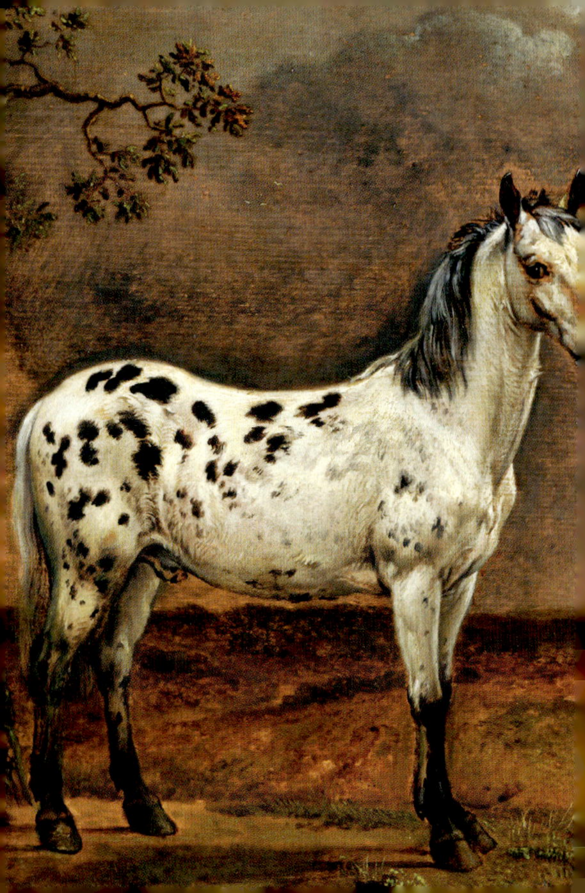

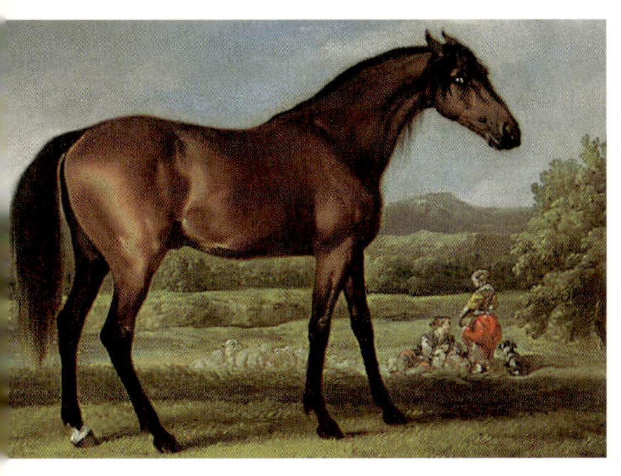

George Stubbs, *Hollyhock*, 1766

Paulus Potter,
The Piebald Horse (detail), 1653

previous double page:
George Stubbs, *Mares and Foals in a River Landscape* (detail), *c.* 1763–68

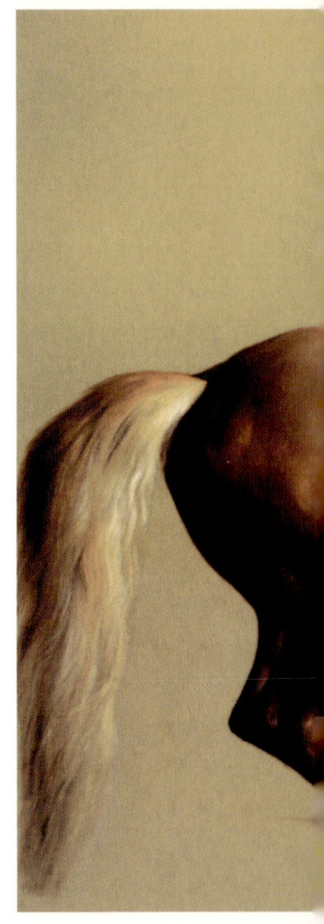

George Stubbs,
Whistlejacket, 1762

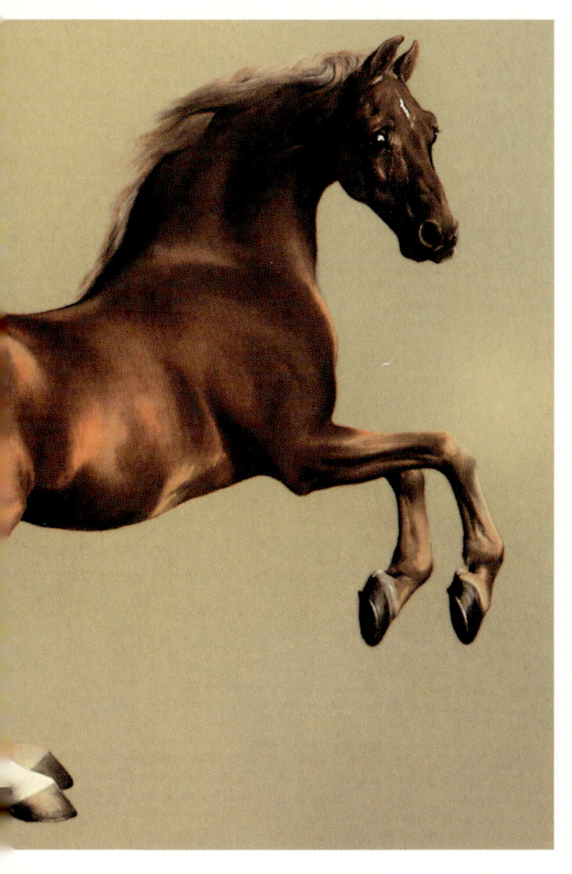

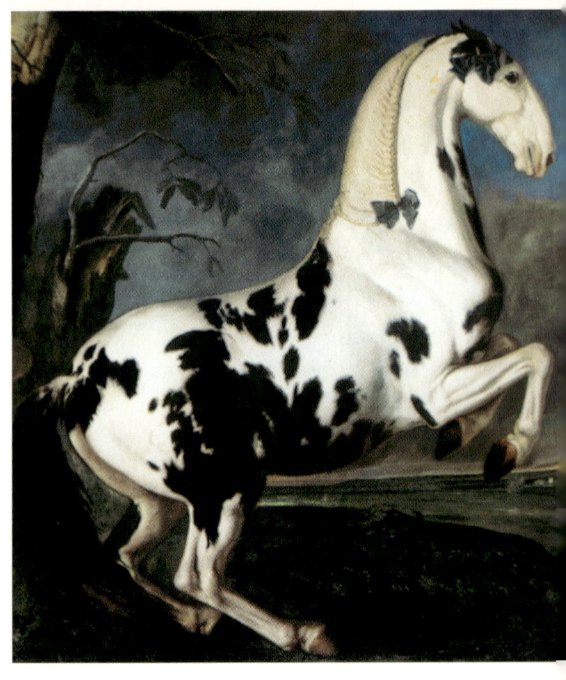

Johann Georg von Hamilton, *Portrait of a Piebald Horse from the Eisgrub Stud*, c. 1700

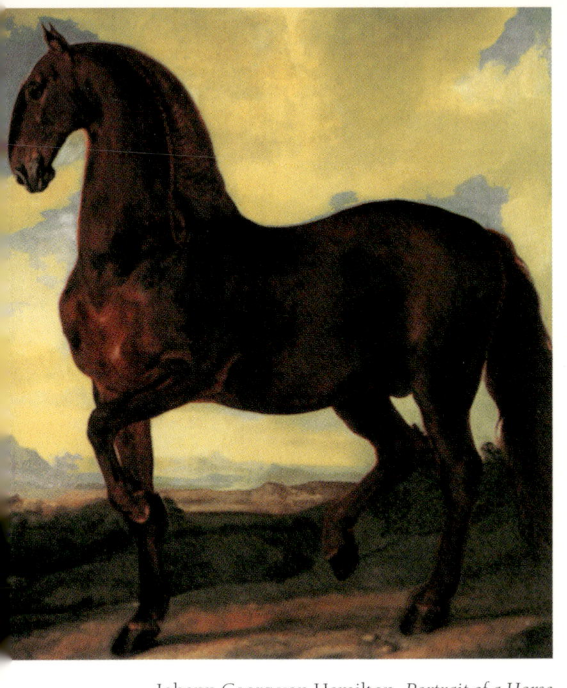

Johann Georg von Hamilton, *Portrait of a Horse from the Eisgrub Stud*, c. 1700

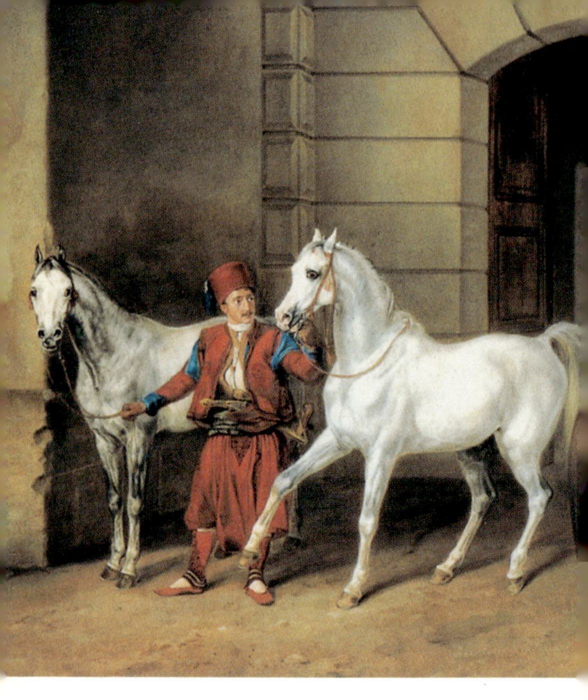

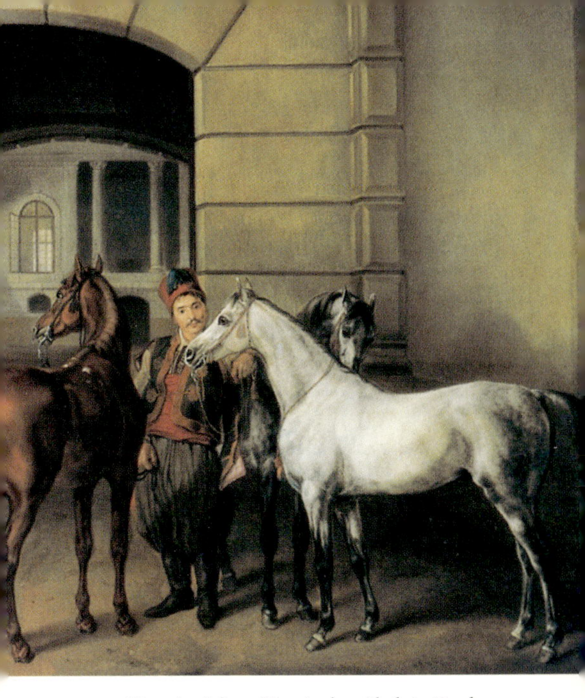

Albrecht Adam, *Five Arabs with their Greek Grooms outside the Royal Mews in Munich*, 1834

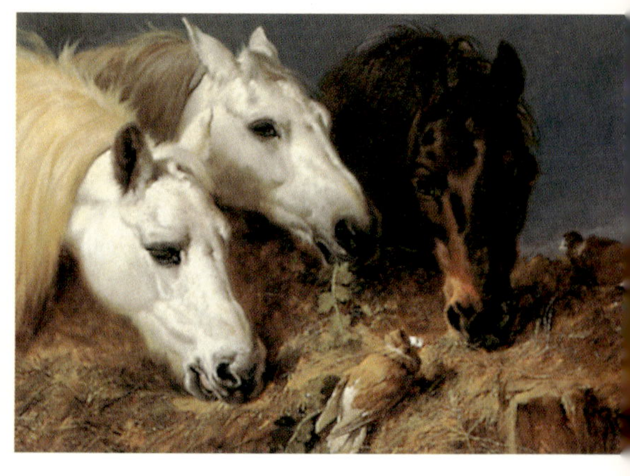

John Frederick Herring, *The Frugal Meal*, *c.* 1847

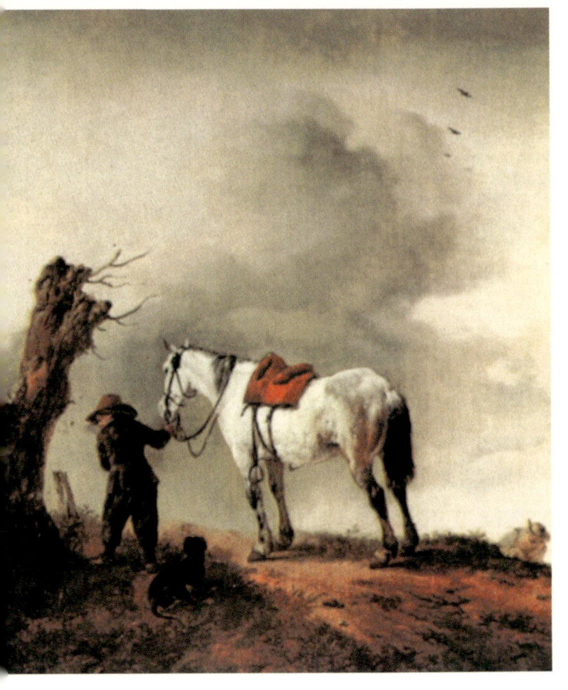

Philips Wouverman, *The Grey*, c. 1646

Théodore Géricault,
Head of a Grey Horse, *c.* 1815

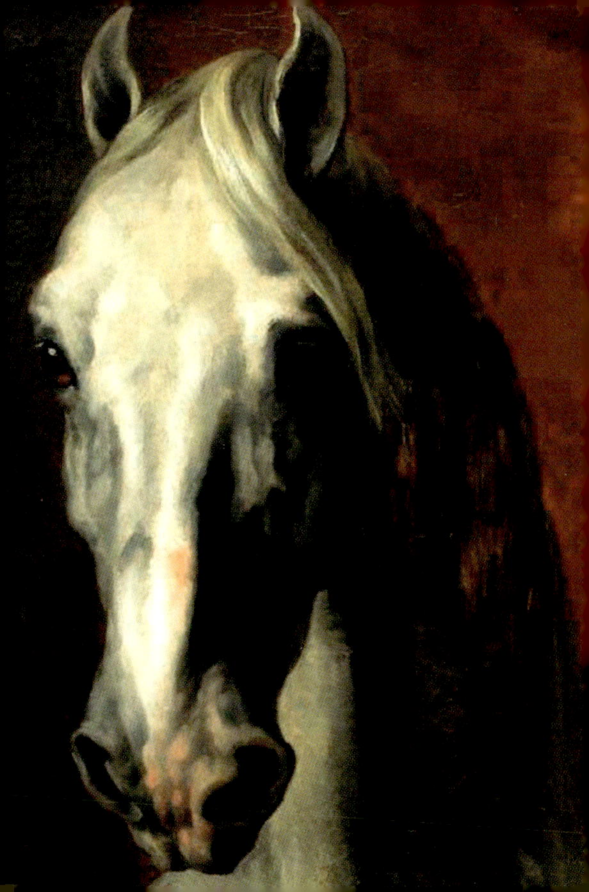

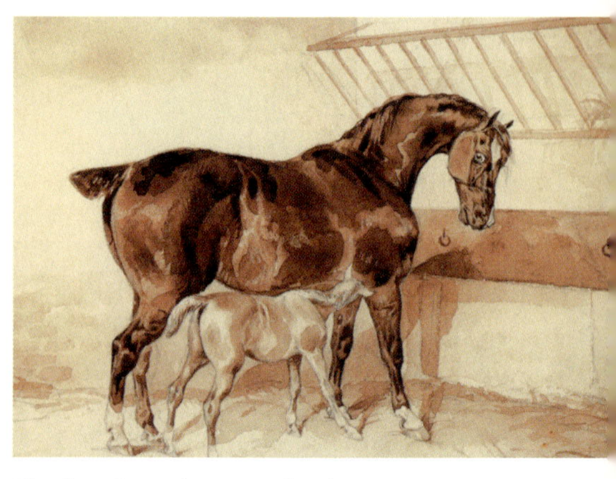

Théodore Géricault, *Mare and Foal*, *c.* 1815

Eugène Delacroix,
Two Horses in a Stable (detail), *c.* 1825

following double page:
Charles Towne, *A Palomino Frightened by an Oncoming Storm, with a Spaniel* (detail), 1814

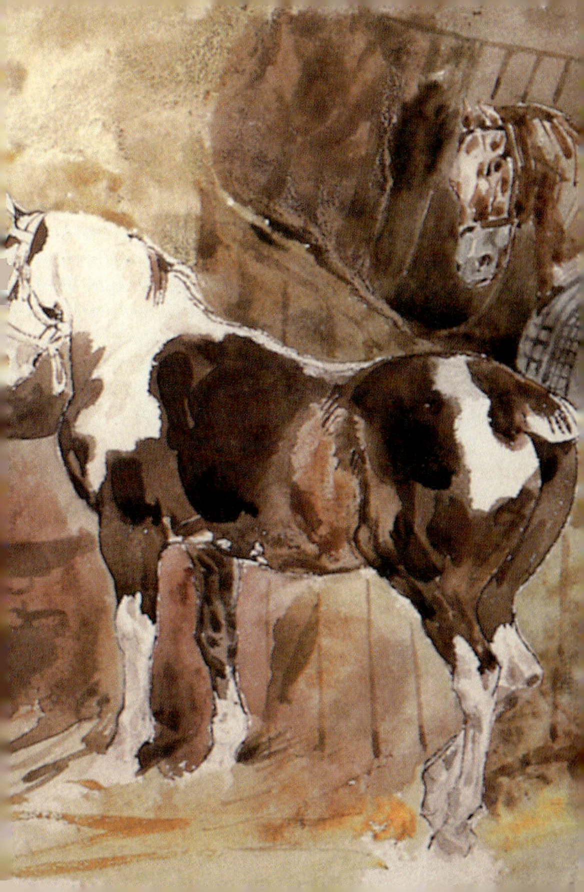

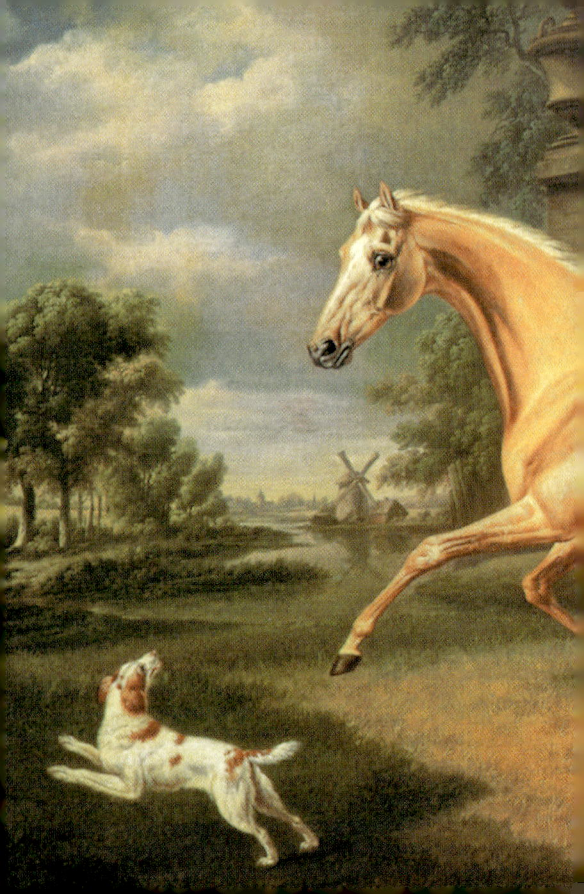

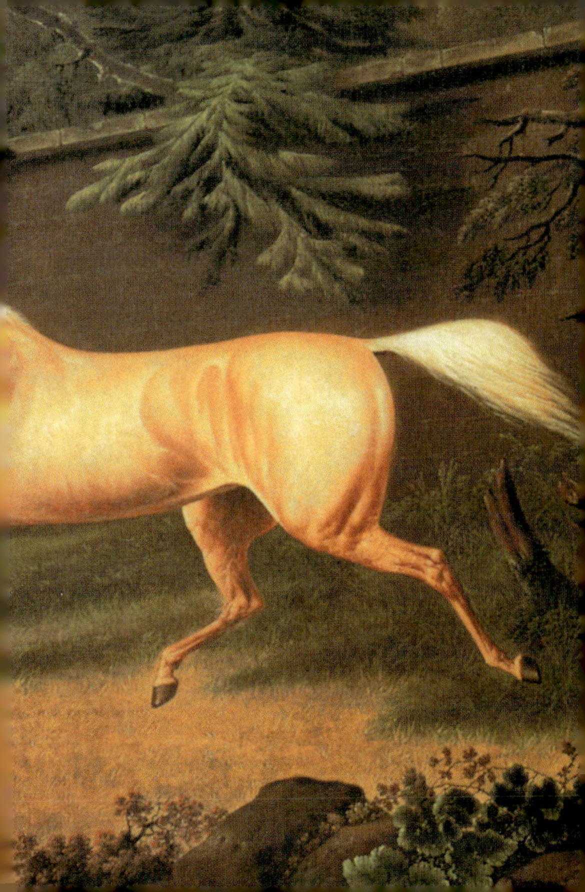

John Wootton,
Racehorses with Jockeys Up by the Rubbing-Down House on Newmarket Heath, c. 1740

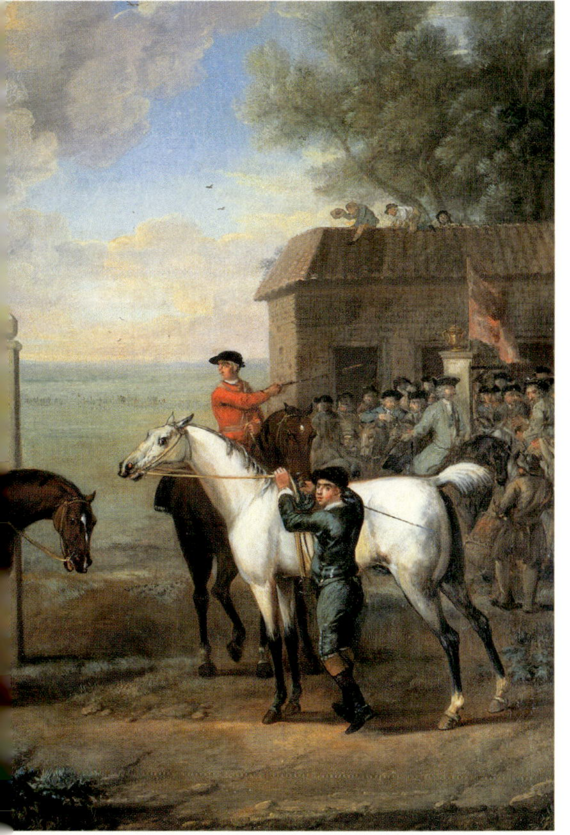

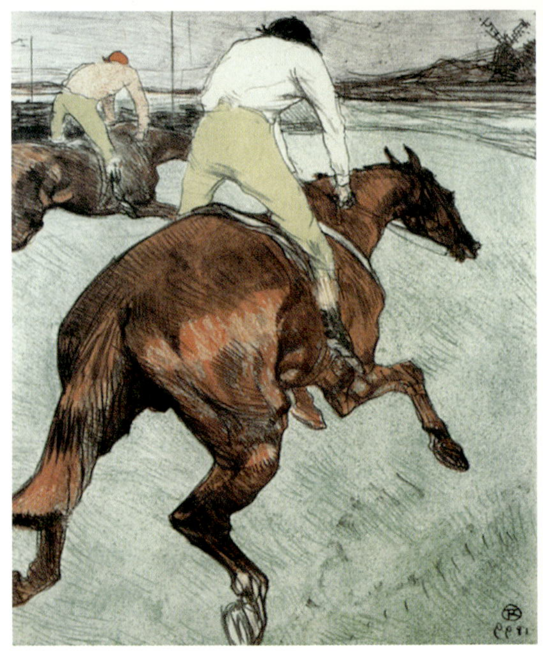

Henri de Toulouse-Lautrec, *The Jockey*, 1899

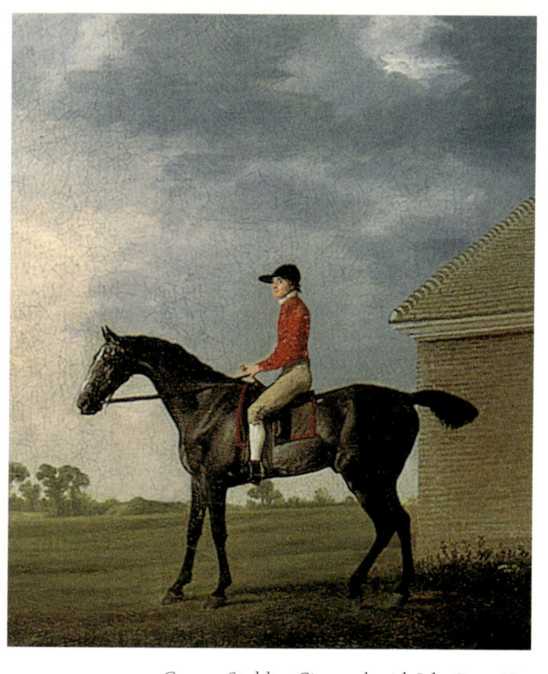

George Stubbs, *Gimcrack with John Pratt Up, at New Market* (detail), *c.* 1765

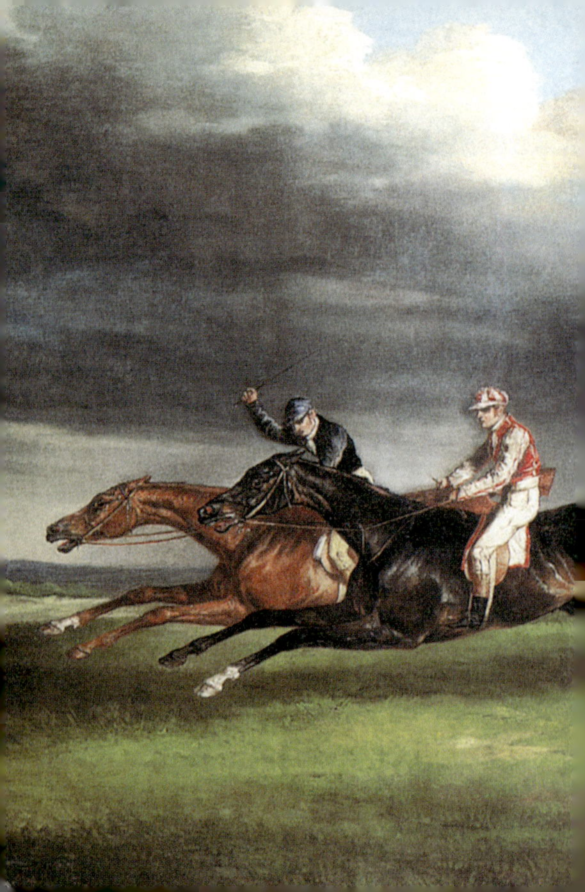

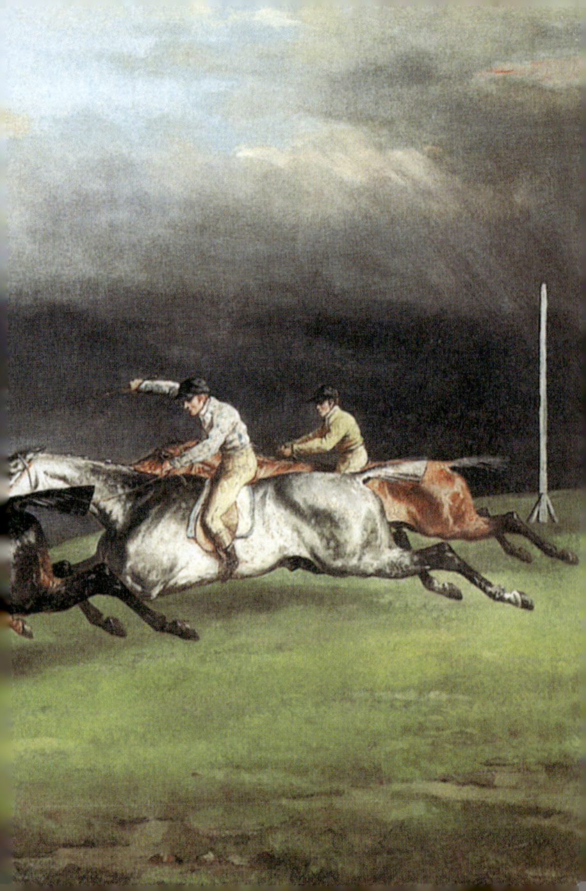

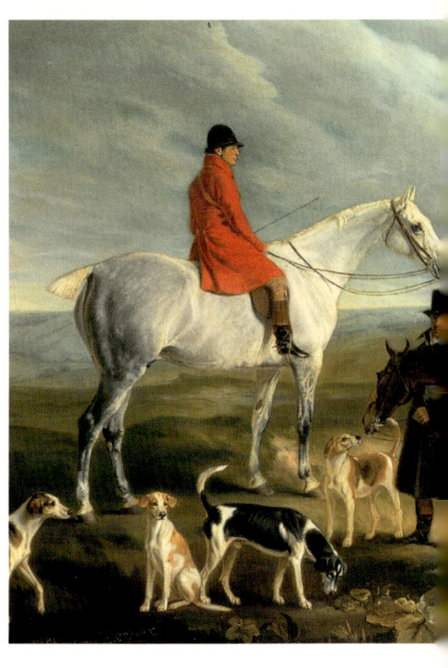

previous double page: Théodore Géricault, *Horse Racing at Epsom 1821*, 1821

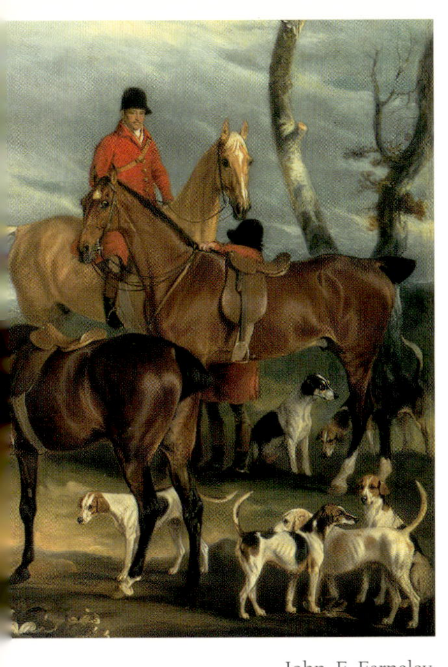

John. E. Ferneley,
The Meet, Melton Mowbray, 1829

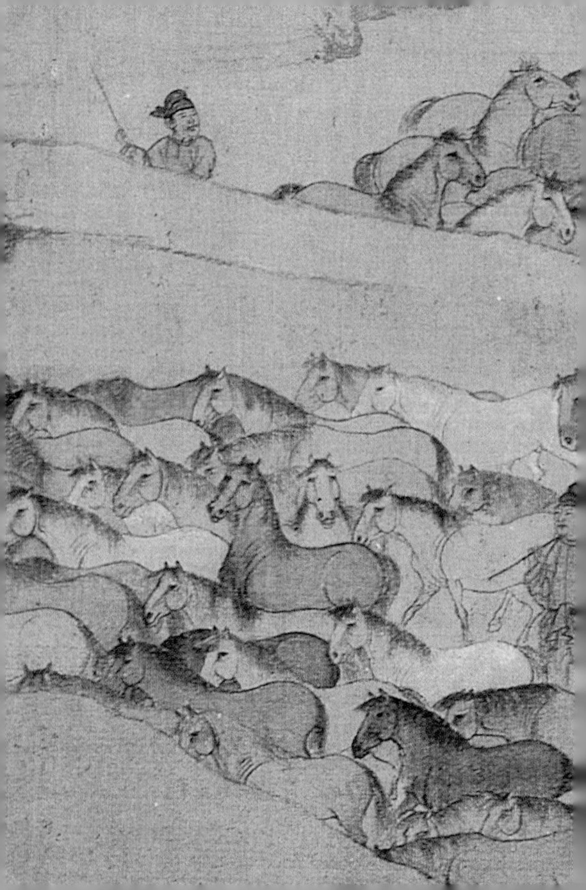

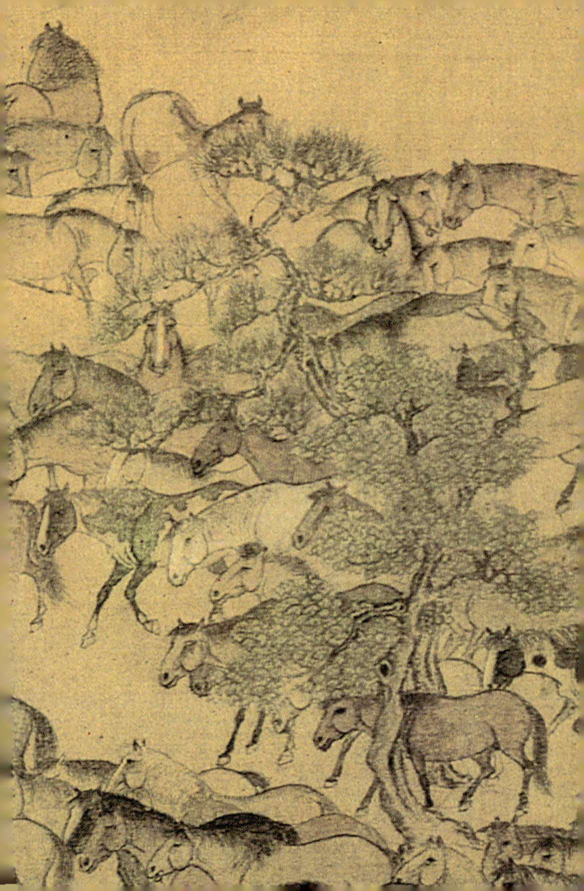

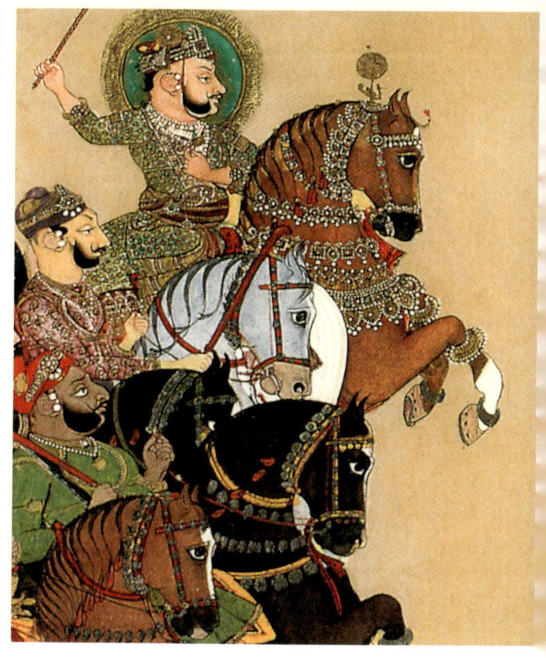

Indian, *Polo Game* (detail), 1838

previous double page:
Li Gonlin, *Herding the Horses* (detail), 11th century

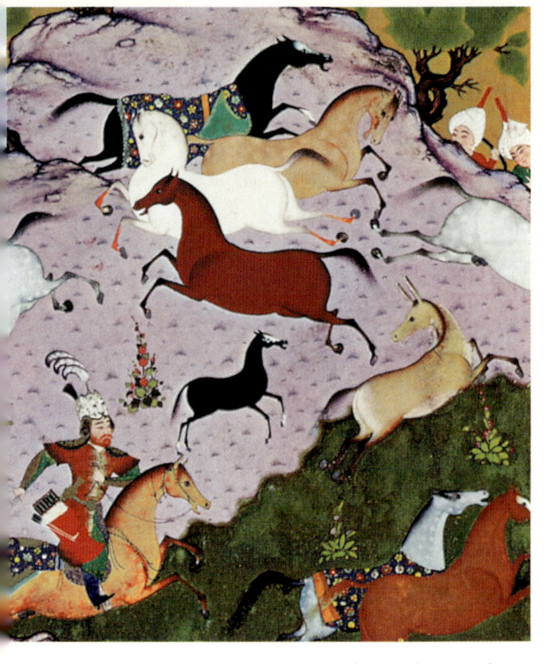

Persian, *Rustem follows the Diw Akwan* (detail), *c.* 1520

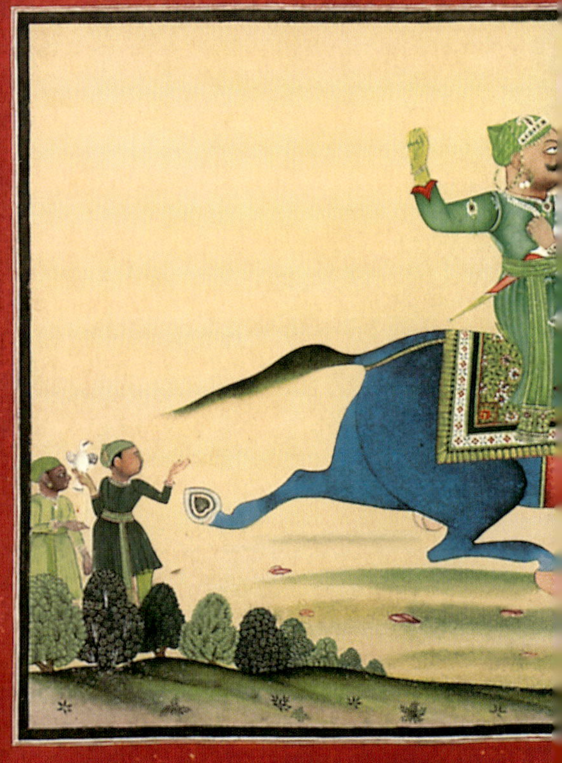

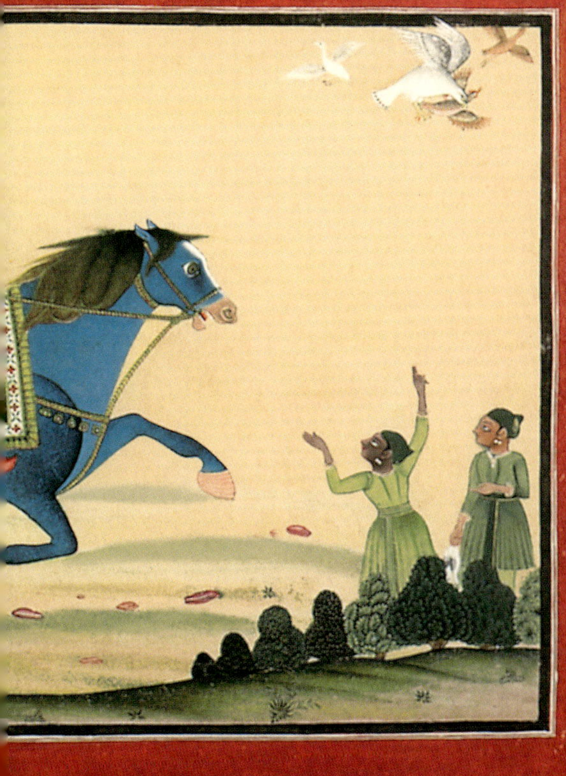

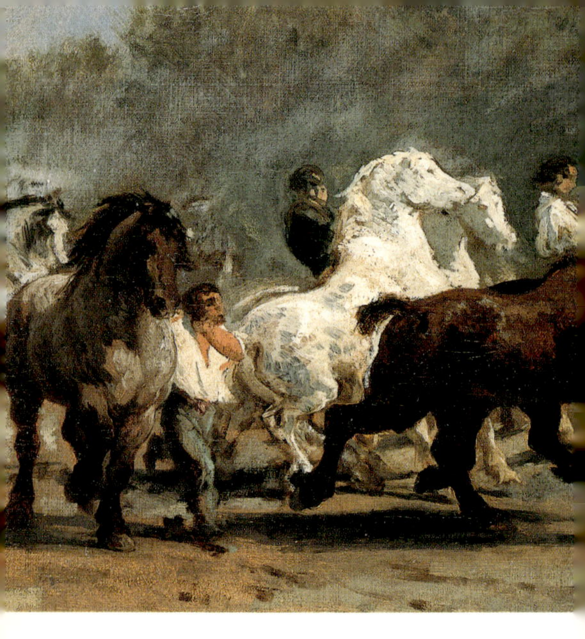

previous double page:
Indian, *Shrimant Patelji Mahadji Sindhia on Horseback out Hawking*, c. 1800

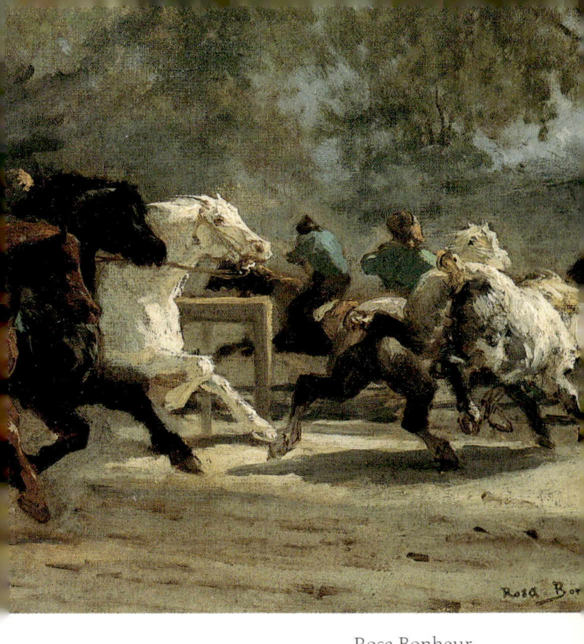

Rosa Bonheur,
Study for *The Horse Market*, 1900

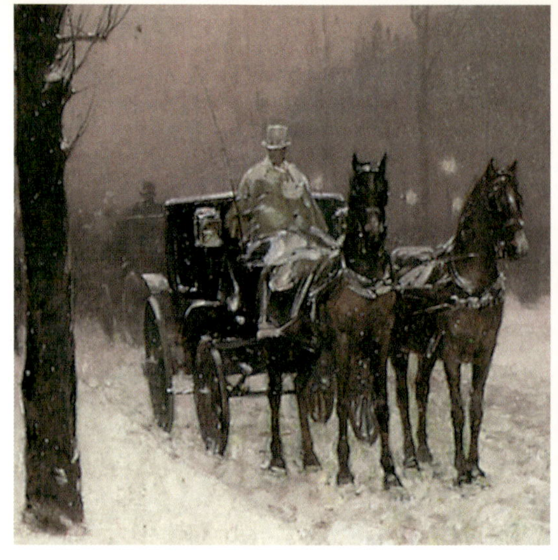

Childe Hassam, *Street Scene with Hansom Cab* (detail), 1887

Rudolf Koller, *The Gotthard Post Coach*, 1873

following double page: Anton Mauve, *Collecting Seaweed* (detail), *c.* 1880

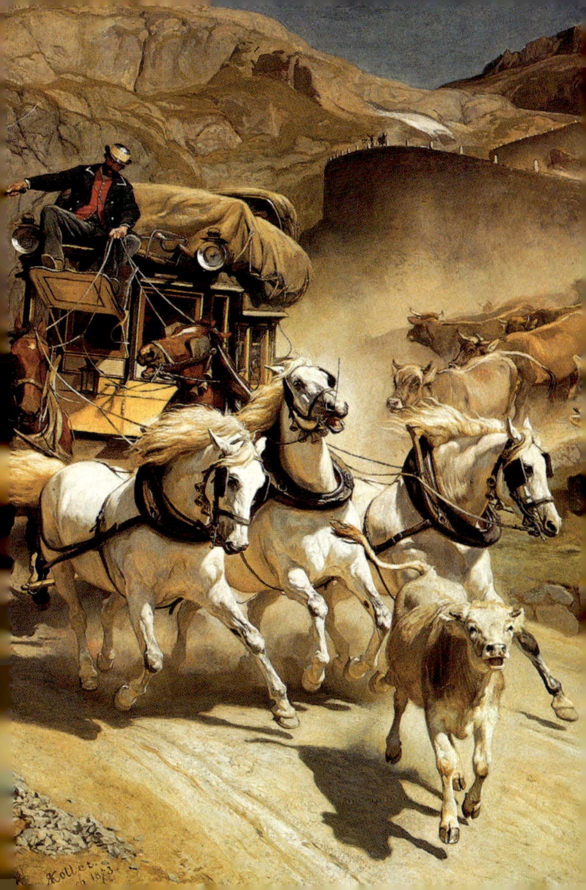
Koller.
1873

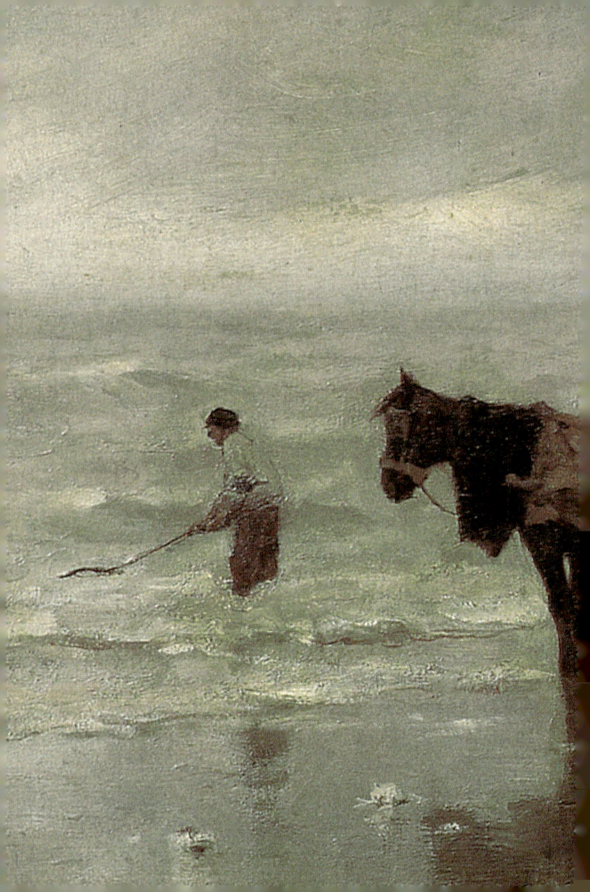

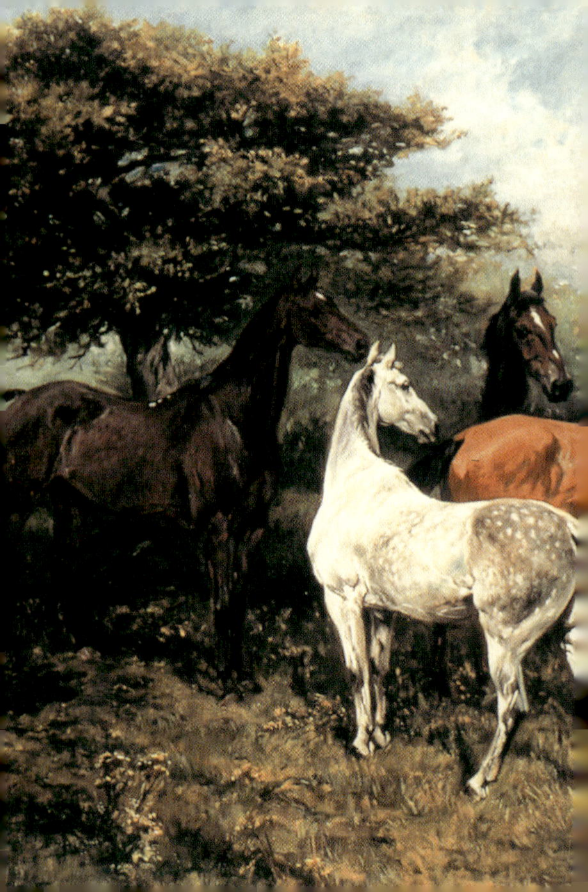

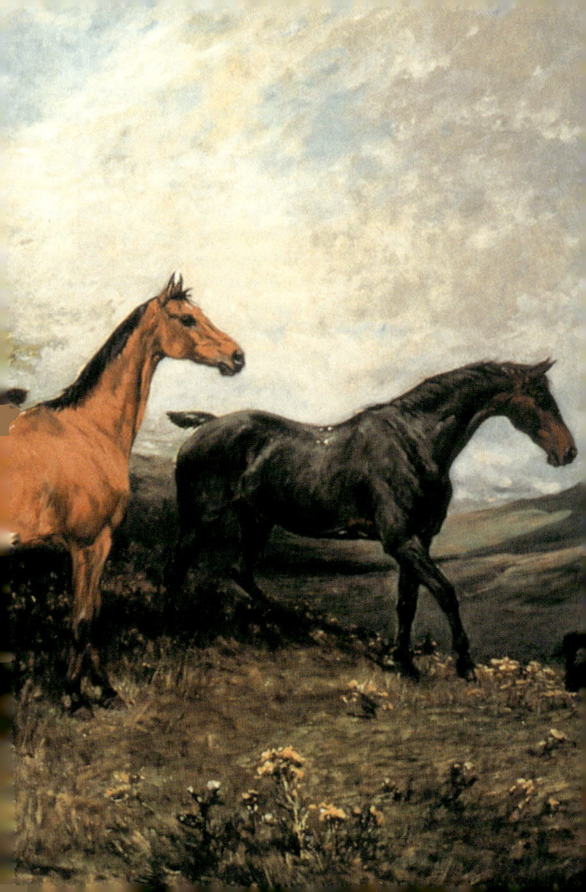

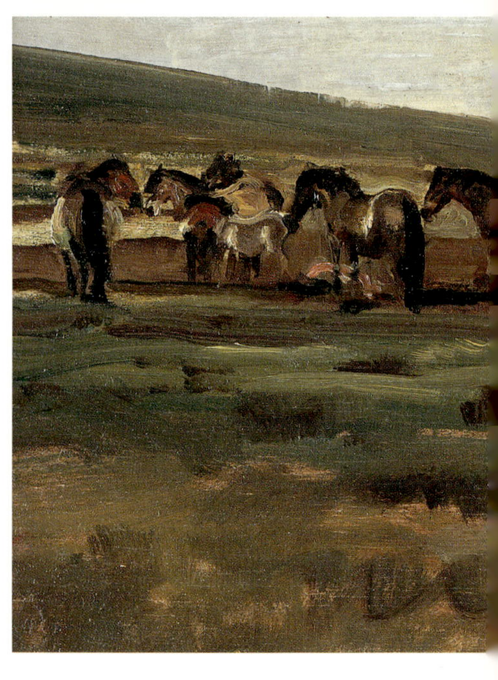

previous double page:
John Emms, *Mares and Foals*, *c.* 1900

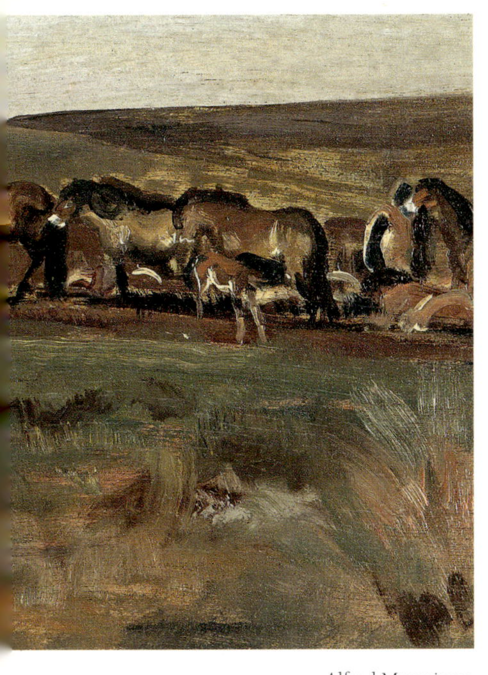

Alfred Munnings,
Exmoor Ponies, Study No. 3, c. 1942

List of Works Illustrated

Page 7:
Detail from 'The Bayeux Tapesty', *c.* 1070, Centre Guillaume le Conquérant, Bayeux, France

Page 10:
The Horses of the Three Kings, early 12th century, painted cassette in church ceiling, Zillis, Switzerland

Pages 14/15:
George Stubbs (1724–1806), *Mares and Foals in a River Landscape* (detail), *c.* 1763–68, oil on canvas, 101.6 x 161.9 cm, Tate Britain, London

Page 16:
Paulus Potter (1625–54), *The Piebald Horse* (detail), 1653, oil on canvas, 30.5 x 41 cm, Musée du Louvre, Paris

Page 17:
George Stubbs (with additions by Joseph Vernet and François Boucher), *Hollyhock*, 1766, oil on canvas, 38.7 x 47.7 cm, The Royal Collection, Windsor Castle, © Her Majesty Queen Elizabeth II

Pages 18/19:
George Stubbs, *Whistlejacket*, 1762, oil on canvas, 292 x 246.4 cm, National Gallery, London

Page 20:
Johann Georg von Hamilton (1672–1737), *Portrait of a Piebald Horse from the Eisgrub Stud*, *c.* 1700, oil on canvas, 258 x 210 cm, The Liechtenstein Museum, Vienna

Page 21:
Johann Georg von Hamilton, *Portrait of a Horse from the Eisgrub Stud*, *c.* 1700, oil on canvas, 260 x 202 cm, The Liechtenstein Museum, Vienna

Pages 22/23:
Albrecht Adam (1786–1862), *Five Arabs with their Greek Grooms outside the Royal Mews in Munich*, 1834, oil on canvas, 63 x 91 cm, private collection

Page 24:
John Frederick Herring (1795–1865), *The Frugal Meal*, *c.* 1847, oil on canvas, 54.6 x 74.9 cm, Tate Britain, London

Page 25:
Philips Wouverman (*c.* 1619–68), *The Grey*, *c.* 1646, oil on panel, Rijksmuseum, Amsterdam

Page 27:
Théodore Géricault (1791–1824), *Head of a Grey Horse*, *c.* 1815, oil on canvas, 65 x 54 cm, Musée du Louvre, Paris

Page 28:
Théodore Géricault, *Mare and Foal*, *c.* 1815, watercolour, private collection

Page 29:
Eugène Delacroix (1798–1863), *Two Horses in a Stable* (detail), *c.* 1825, watercolour, 18.4 x 26.5 cm, private collection

Pages 30/31:
Charles Towne (1763–1840), *A Palomino Frightened by an Oncoming Storm, with a Spaniel* (detail), 1814, oil on canvas, 76 x 59 cm, private collection

Pages 32/33:
John Wootton (1686–1765), *Racehorses with Jockeys Up by the Rubbing-Down House on Newmarket Heath*, *c.* 1740, oil on canvas, private collection, courtesy Christie's Images, London

Page 34:
Henri de Toulouse-Lautrec (1864–1901), *The Jockey*, 1899, lithograph on paper, 51.5 x 3 cm, The Brooklyn Museum

Page 35:
George Stubbs, *Gimcrack with John Pratt Up, at New Market* (detail), *c.* 1765, oil on canvas, 100.4 x 127 cm, Fitzwilliam Museum, Cambridge

Pages 36/37:
Théodore Géricault, *Horse Racing at Epsom 1821*, 1821, oil on canvas, 92 x 123 cm, Musée du Louvre

Pages 38/39:
John. E. Ferneley (1781–1860), *The Meet, Melton Mowbray*, 1829, oil on canvas, private collection, courtesy of the British Sporting Art Trust

Pages 40/41:
Li Gonlin (1049–1106), *Herding the Horses, after Wei Yan* (detail), 11th century, pen and ink and wash, on silk, scroll 46.2 x 429.8 cm, Palace Museum, Beijing

Page 42:
Indian, *Maharao ram Singh playing Polo near Gagraon* (detail), 1838, opaque watercolour, gold, metallic grey water-colour, 61 x 74.6 cm, Rao Madho Singh Trust Museum, Fort Kotah

Page 43:
Persian, *Rustem follows the Diw Akwan* (detail),

c. 1520, miniature from *The Book of Kings*, The Metropolitan Museum, New York

Pages 44/45:
Indian, *Shrimant Patelji Mahadji Sindhia on Horseback out Hawking*, *c.* 1800, opaque water-colour and gold, 36.1 x 51.4 cm, Rao Madho Singh Trust Museum, Fort Kotah

Pages 46/47:
Rosa Bonheur (1822–99), Study for *The Horse Market*, 1900, oil on canvas, 28 x 61 cm, private collection, courtesy of Thomas Brod and Patrick Pilkington

Page 48:
Childe Hassam (1859–1935), *Street Scene with Hansom Cab* (detail), 1887, oil on canvas, 43.2 x 78.7 cm, private collection

Page 49:
Rudolf Koller (1828–1905), *The Gotthard Post Coach*, 1873, oil on canvas, 117 x 100 cm, Kunsthaus, Zurich

Pages 50/51:
Anton Mauve (1838–1888), *Collecting Seaweed*, *c.* 1880, oil on canvas, 51 x 71 cm, Musée d'Orsay, Paris

Pages 52/53:
John Emms (1844–1912), *Mares and Foals*, *c.* 1900, oil on canvas, private collection

Pages 54/55:
Alfred Munnings (1878–1959), *Exmoor Ponies, Study No. 3*, *c.* 1942 , oil on panel, 16.5 x 24 cm, private collection, courtesy Bonhams, London

Cover: George Stubbs, *Whistlejacket* (detail), see pages 18/19
Inside front cover and title page: Alfred Munnings, *Exmoor Ponies, Study No. 3* (detail), see pages 54/55
Page 2: Rudolf Koller, *The Gotthard Post Coach* (detail), see page 49

Picture credits: akg: p. 16, Artothek, Weilheim: p. 49,
The Bridgeman Art Library: pp. Front Cover, 1, 18/19, 32/33, 38/39, 46/47, 54/55

The Library of Congress Cataloguing-in-Publication data is available; British Library Cataloguing-in-Publication Data: a catalogue record for this book is available from the British Library; Deutsche Bibliothek holds a record of this publication in the Deutsche Nationalbibliografie; detailed bibliographical data can be found under: http://dnb.ddb.de

Series title and concept: Jürgen Tesch
Concept and picture selection for this book: Christopher Wynne

© Prestel Verlag, Munich · Berlin · London · New York, 2005

Prestel Verlag, Königinstrasse 9, 80539 Munich
Tel. +49 (89) 38 17 09-0; Fax +49 (89) 38 17 09-35

Prestel Publishing Ltd., 4 Bloomsbury Place, London WC1A 2QA
Tel. +44 (020) 7323-5004; Fax +44 (020) 7636-8004

Prestel Publishing, 900 Broadway, Suite 603, New York, NY 10003
Tel. +1 (212) 995-2720; Fax +1 (212) 995-2733
www.prestel.com

Copy-edited by Rosie Jackson
Design and layout: Florian Tutte
Origination: ReproLine Genceller, Munich
Printing: Jütte-Messedruck, Leipzig
Binding: Kunst- und Verlagsbinderei, Leipzig

Printed in Germany on acid-free paper

ISBN 3-7913-3465-4